For you, mamma

FriesenPress

One Printers Way
Altona, MB R0G 0B0
Canada

www.friesenpress.com

Copyright © 2023 by Frida Backlund
First Edition — 2023

All rights reserved.

Illustrations by Sasha Baines

No part of this publication may be reproduced in any form, or by any means, electronic or mechanical, including photocopying, recording, or any information browsing, storage, or retrieval system, without permission in writing from FriesenPress.

ISBN
978-1-03-915143-7 (Hardcover)
978-1-03-915142-0 (Paperback)
978-1-03-915144-4 (eBook)

1. JUVENILE NONFICTION, SOCIAL TOPICS, DEATH & DYING

Distributed to the trade by The Ingram Book Company

Our Guardian Angels

WRITTEN BY
FRIDA BACKLUND

ILLUSTRATED BY
SASHA BAINES

When you feel lonely and the world seems unfair,
you may be missing someone who was special and rare.

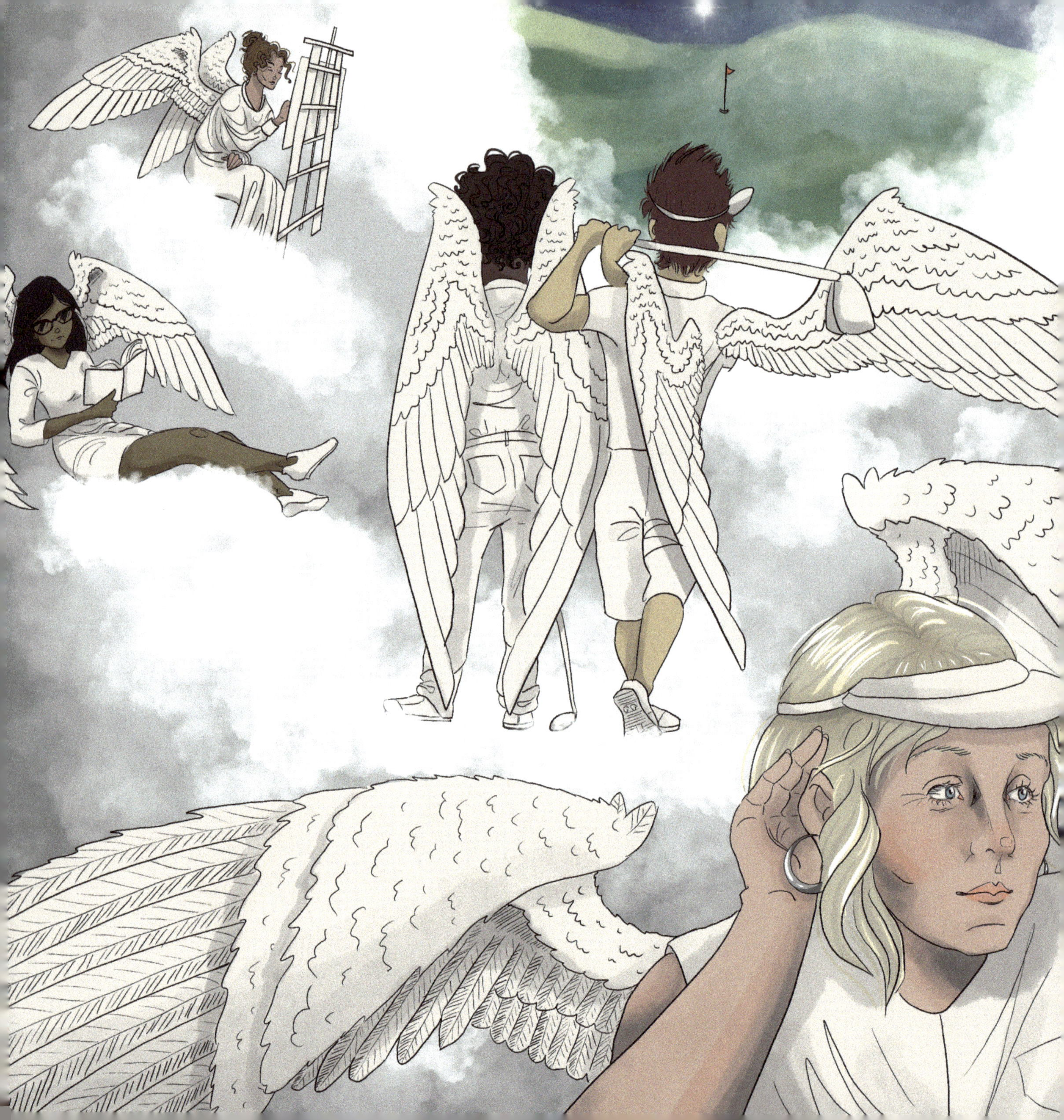

High up in the sky where all the angels fly,
the one looking over you hears when you cry.

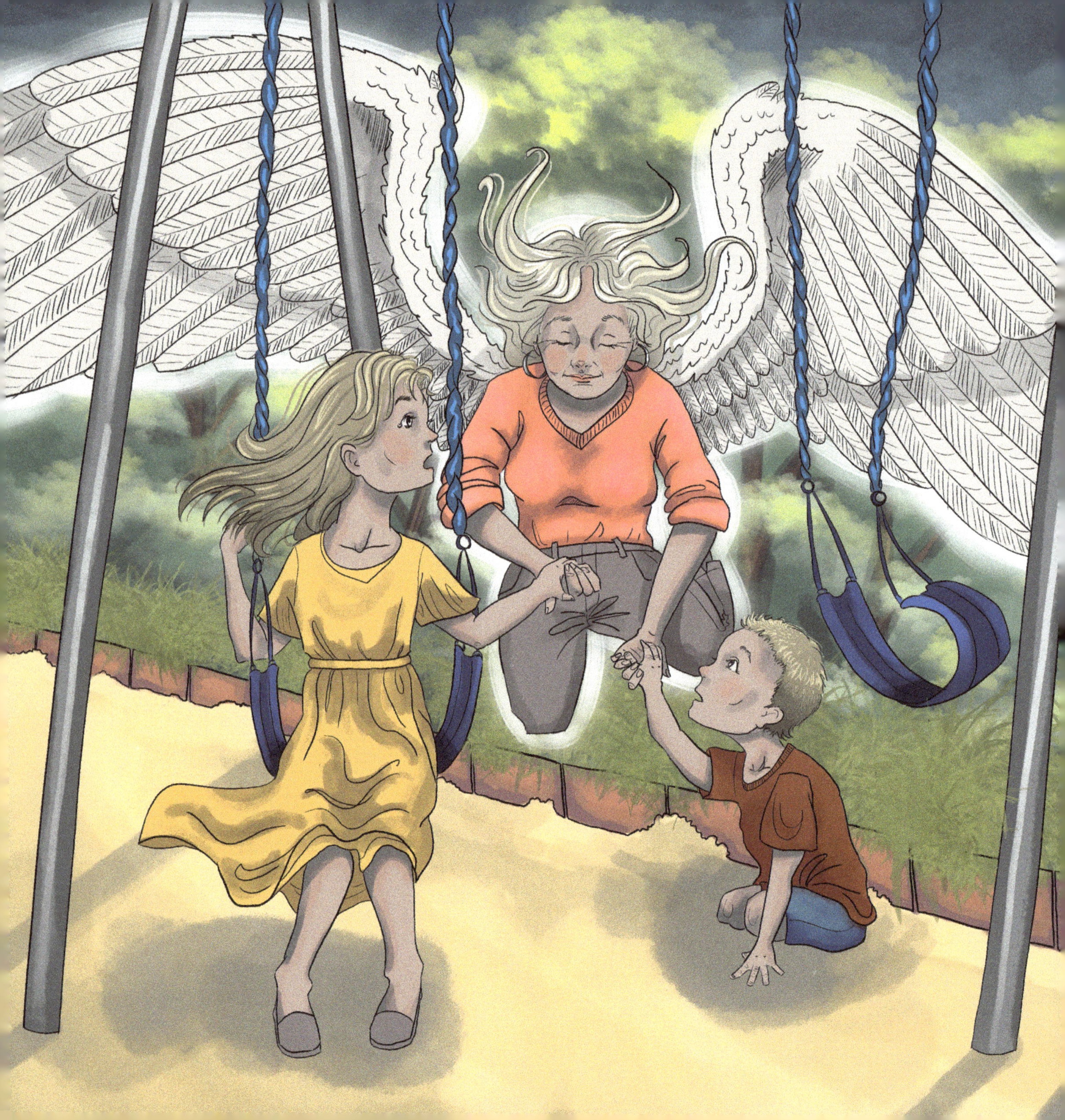

Your angel will fly down quicker than quick,
and sooth the bad feeling, brick by brick.

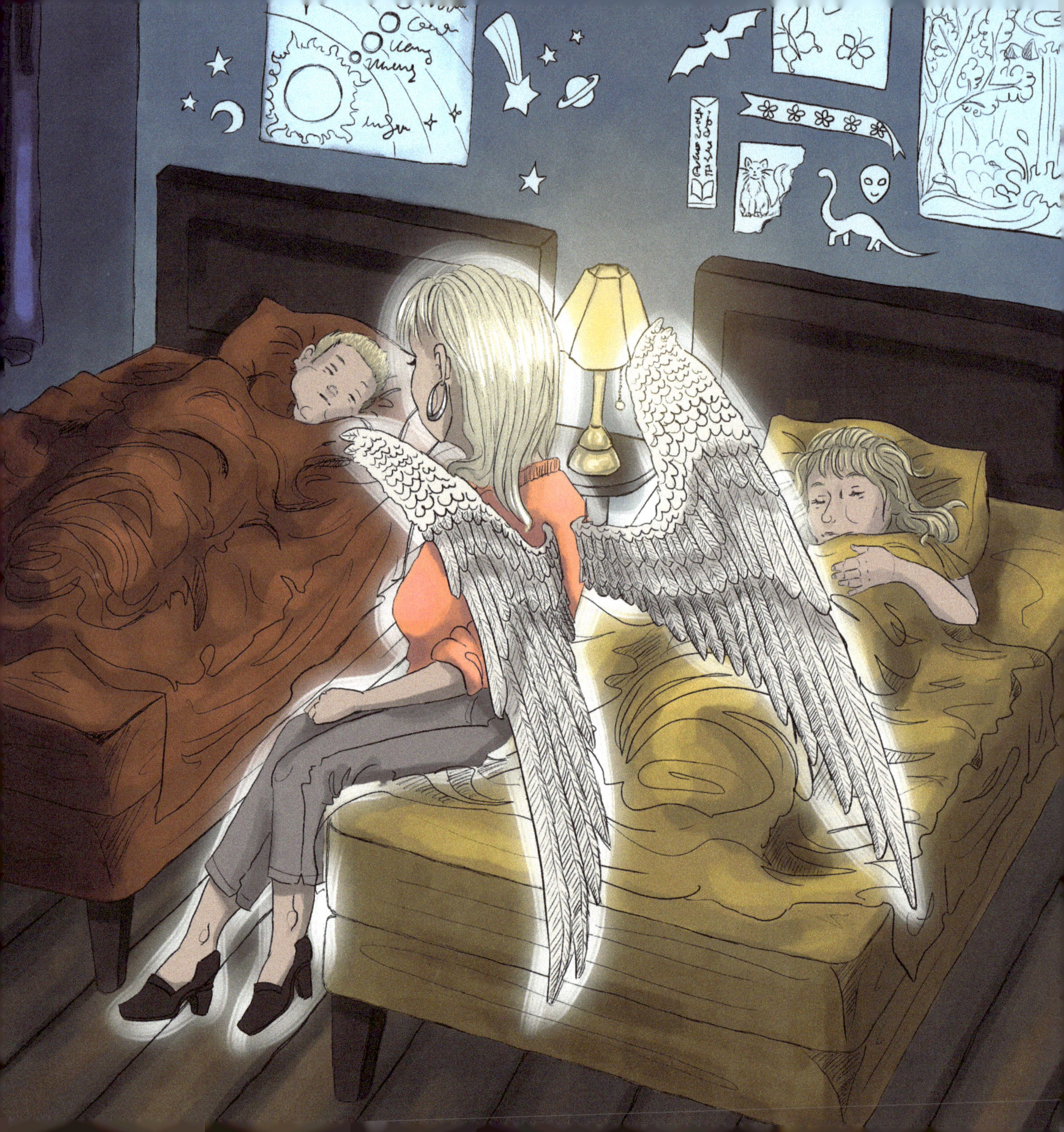

They will sit by your bed and stay close to you
to make you feel better, because they miss you, too.

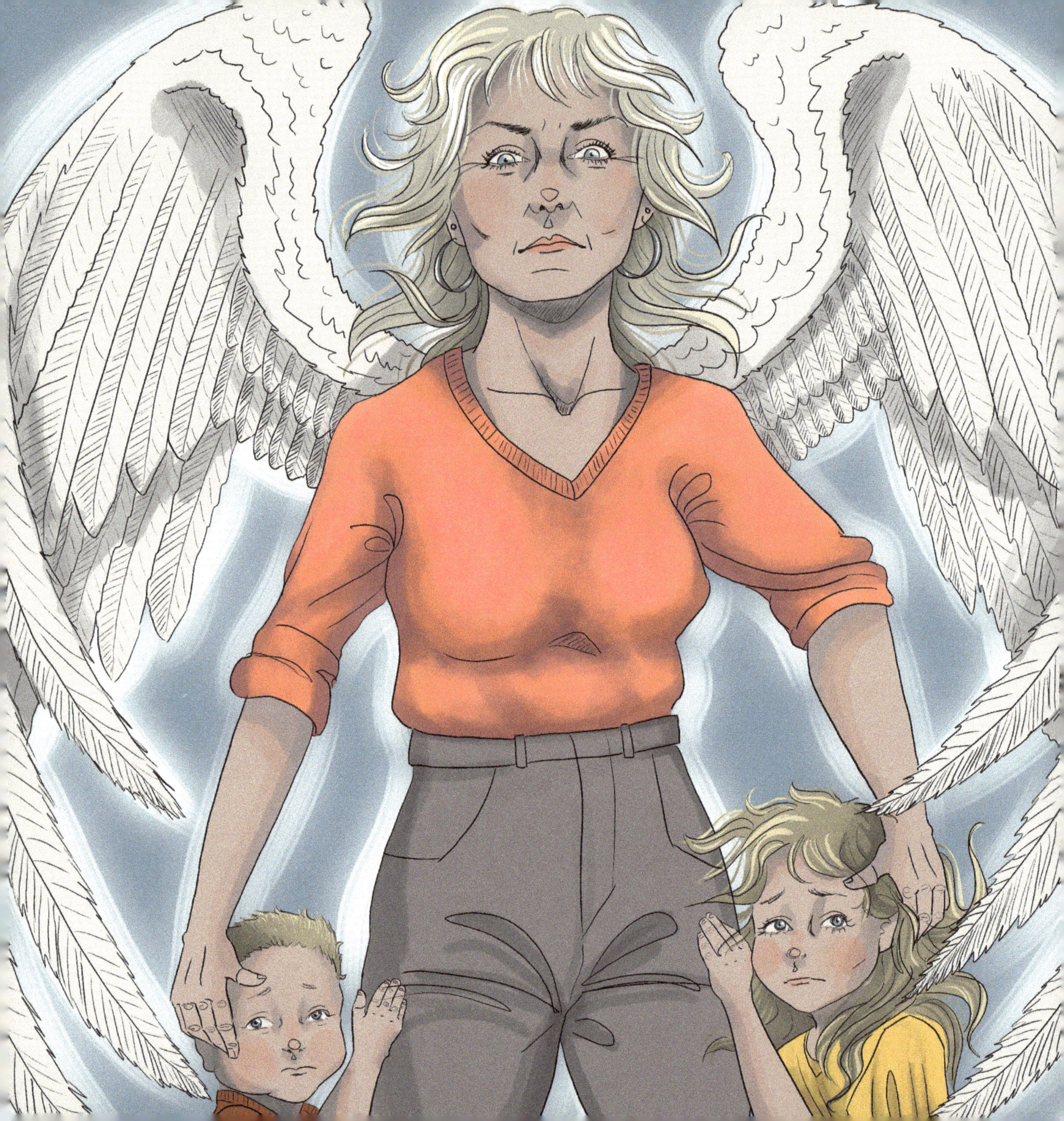

They will protect you with their mighty wings,
and stand beside you as you experience hard things.

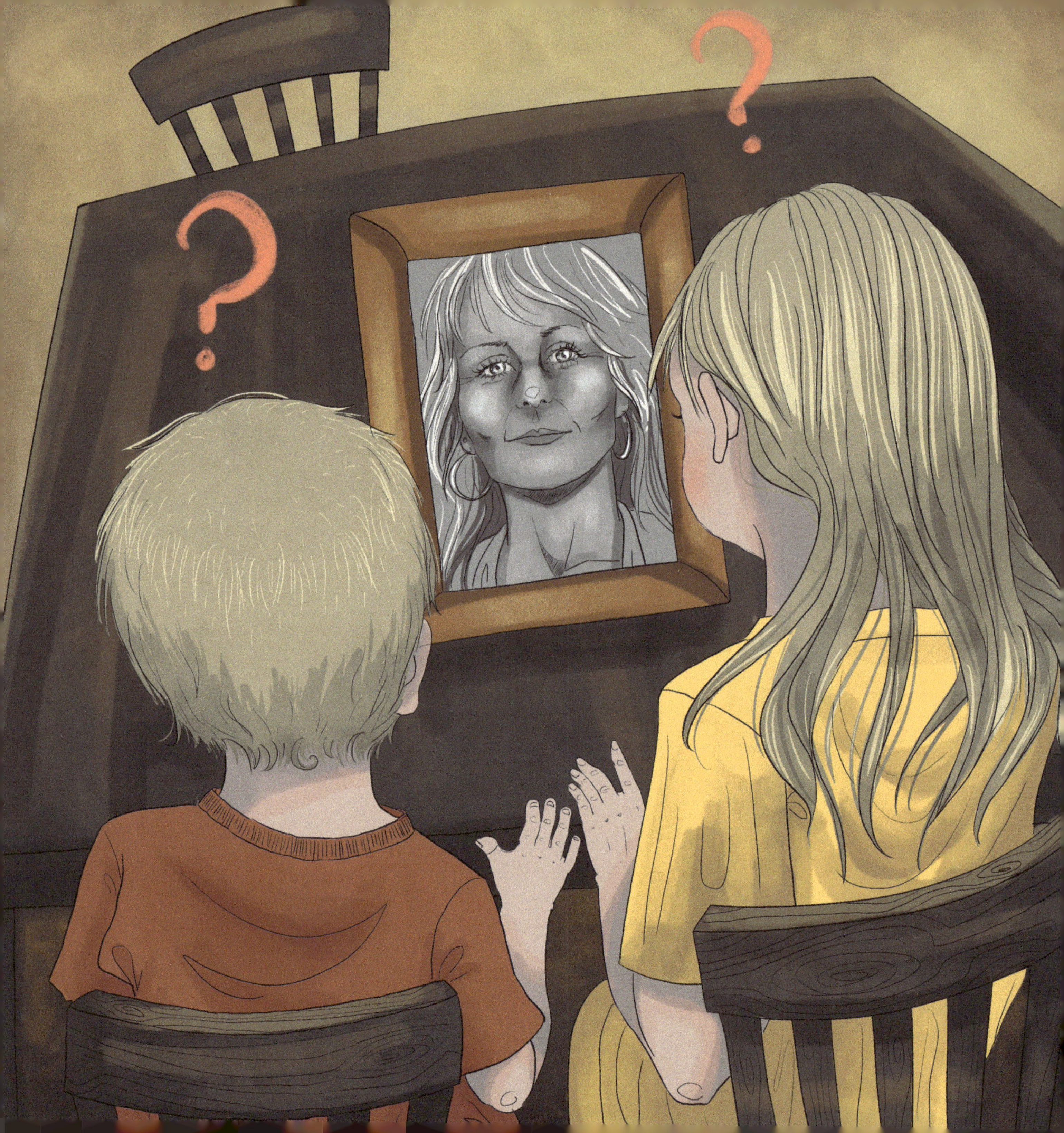

They will be your guardian wherever you are—
no matter the time, no matter how far.

When you miss someone, you might not understand why
they had to leave you to go home to the sky.

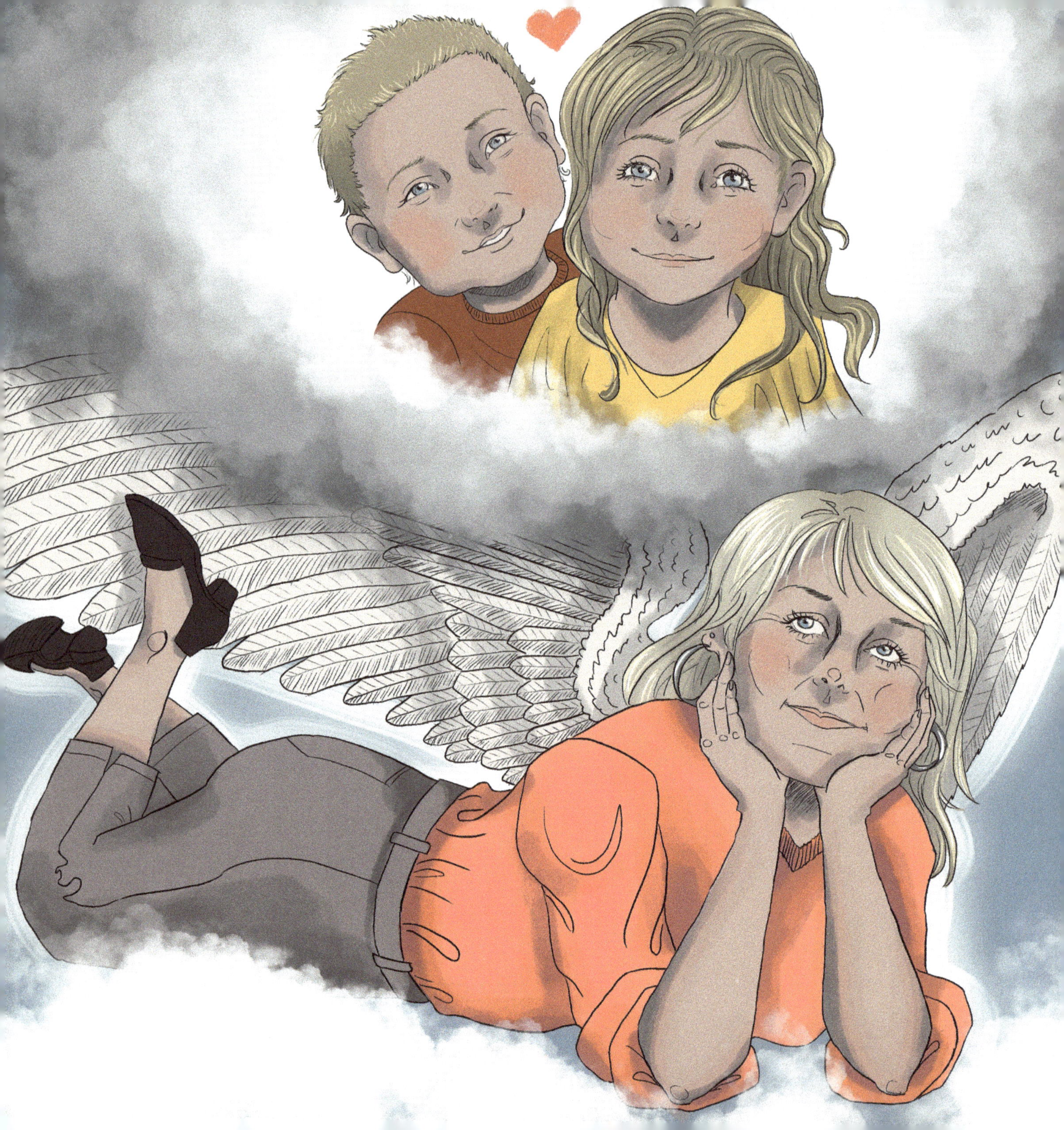

But remember, even if they can't wipe your tears,
They are still with you, and will help ease your fears.

They love you, they care, and they are always near,
your guardian angel, with you year after year.

CPSIA information can be obtained
at www.ICGtesting.com
Printed in the USA
BVHW010816030323
659600BV00002B/8

9 781039 151420